MATCH OF T...

Colour your
shirt in

Shirt
number

D0811416

This book belongs to		Age
My favourite team is		
My favourite player is		
My highlight of 2021 was		

MATCH of the DAY
WELCOME!

Don't forget to watch MOTD on BBC One!

2021 WAS A WILD time for football, packed with highs and lows that made it a year to remember. This book captures all the big moments – the heroes, the goals, the games and more. Hope you enjoy it!

All stats correct up to 28 July 2021

WHAT'S IN YOUR MOTD MAG

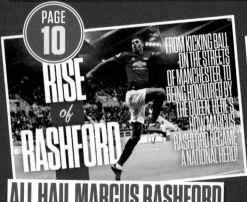

CHAMPIONS City cruised to the title, finishing 12 points clear!

Watch Prem highlights on MOTD, Saturday evenings, on BBC One

BBC one

THE BIG WINNERS OF 2021!

MAN. CITY PREMIER LEAGUE CHAMPIONS

City won their fifth Prem title with three matches to spare. It was also the club's third title in the last four seasons!

HARRY KANE PREMIER LEAGUE GOLDEN BOOT

Kane's 23 goals saw him beat Mohamed Salah to the top spot – it was Kane's third Golden Boot win, but his first since 2016-17!

LEICESTER FA CUP WINNERS

The Foxes' victory over Chelsea at Wembley was their first FA Cup final win, having been runners-up on four previous occasions!

CHELSEA CHAMPIONS LEAGUE WINNERS

Chelsea beat Man. City 1–0 in an all-English final, which was played at the awesome Estadio Do Dragao in Porto, Portugal!

ITALY EURO 2020 WINNERS

Football almost came home, but the Italians won their first major trophy since the 2006 World Cup after defeating England on penalties!

ANNUAL?

96 pages of footy fun! 😍

WHAT'S THAT

The GREATEST EVER photos of ballers with bandages (or other stupid hats) on their head!

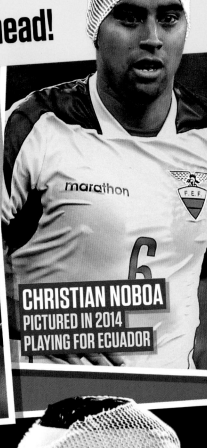

CHRISTIAN NOBOA
PICTURED IN 2014
PLAYING FOR ECUADOR

MATTHIJS DE LIGT
PICTURED IN 2020
PLAYING FOR JUVENTUS

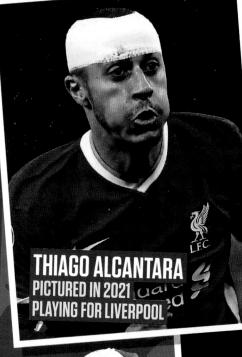

THIAGO ALCANTARA
PICTURED IN 2021
PLAYING FOR LIVERPOOL

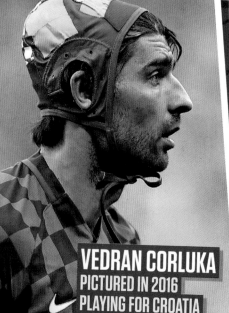

VEDRAN CORLUKA
PICTURED IN 2016
PLAYING FOR CROATIA

ROBIN KNOCHE
PICTURED IN 2018
PLAYING FOR WOLFSBURG

SERVET CETIN
PICTURED IN 2008
PLAYING FOR GALATASARAY

ON YA HEAD?

BENEDIKT HOWEDES
PICTURED IN 2019
PLAYING FOR LOKOMOTIV MOSCOW

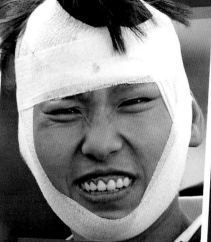

HAN PENG
PICTURED IN 2015
PLAYING FOR CHINA WOMEN

KLAUS GJASULA
PICTURED IN 2019
PLAYING FOR PADERBORN

TOBY ALDERWEIRELD
PICTURED IN 2020
PLAYING FOR TOTTENHAM

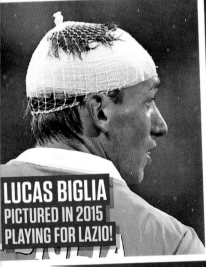

LUCAS BIGLIA
PICTURED IN 2015
PLAYING FOR LAZIO!

ARMANDO IZZO
PICTURED IN 2021
PLAYING FOR TORINO

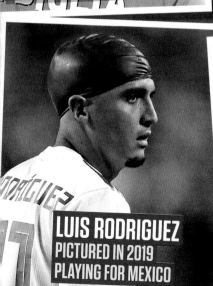

LUIS RODRIGUEZ
PICTURED IN 2019
PLAYING FOR MEXICO

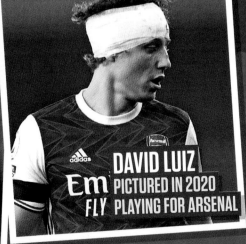

DAVID LUIZ
PICTURED IN 2020
PLAYING FOR ARSENAL

GARY CAHILL
PICTURED IN 2017
PLAYING FOR CHELSEA

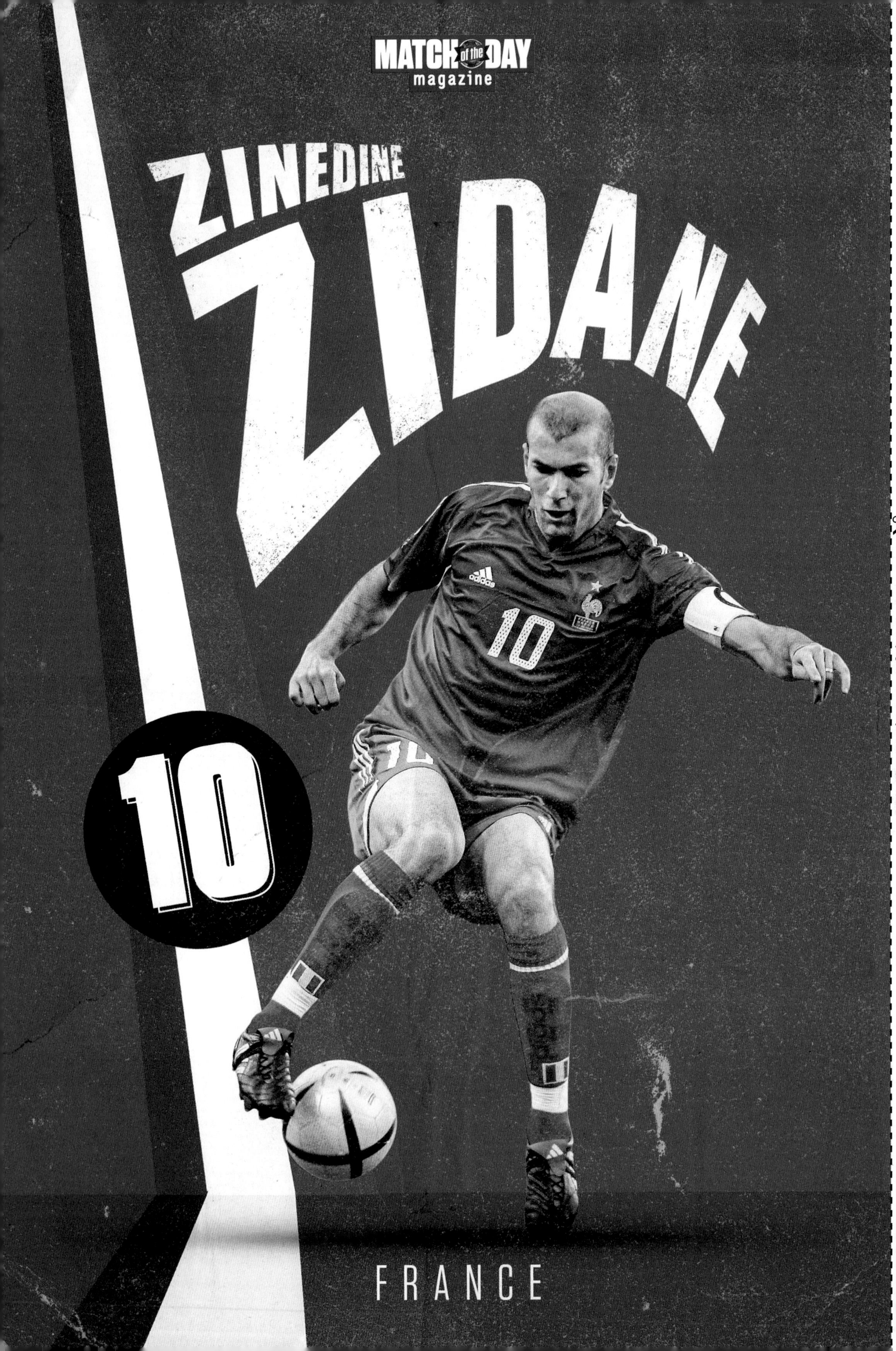
MATCH of the DAY magazine
ZINEDINE
ZIDANE
10
FRANCE

WHO IS OLDER?

HOW DID YOU DO? TURN TO p92 FOR THE ANSWERS!

A very simple challenge for you – just tell us who you think is the oldest of the two options!

1

Cristiano Ronaldo | Wayne Rooney

2

Rihanna | Troy Deeney

3

Jurgen Klopp | Jacob Rees-Mogg

4

Lucas Moura | Taylor Swift

5

Zlatan Ibrahimovic | Holly Willoughby

6

John Stones | Ariana Grande

The RISE of RASHFORD

FROM KICKING BALL ON THE STREETS OF MANCHESTER, TO BEING HONOURED BY THE QUEEN, HERE'S HOW MARCUS RASHFORD BECAME A NATIONAL HERO!

TURN OVER FOR MORE!

BEGINNINGS!

Marcus was born on 31 October, 1997, in Manchester, just a few months after Sir Alex Ferguson lifted his fourth league title with Man. United. He grew up with four older siblings and lived with his mum Melanie, who worked multiple jobs to feed the family!

IDOL!

No joke, Rashy started his footy life at five years old as a keeper for Fletcher Moss Rangers – his idol was Tim Howard, Man. United's No.1 at the time!

THE EVOLUTION OF MARCUS

JULY 2014

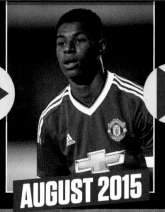

AUGUST 2015

SEPTEMBER 2016

MARCH 2017

ENGLAND!

On 27 May 2016, Marcus started in a Euro 2016 warm-up match against Australia at the Stadium Of Light and banged in the opening goal of a 2–1 win after just three minutes, becoming the youngest English baller to score on his international debut!

BIG DECISION!

At the age of seven, after leading his club to victory in a tournament, both Manchester clubs were chasing Marcus' signature. He trained with City, but chose United. He was so good, he was fast-tracked through the youth system and he ended up training with Paul Pogba and Jesse Lingard, who were five years older!

TROPHIES!

Despite being only 23, Rashy's trophy cabinet started to fill up. On his honours' list is an FA Cup, EFL Cup, Community Shield, Europa League and Man. United's Goal of The Season award from 2019-20!

DEBUT!

On 25 February 2016, in a Europa League tie against Danish club Midtjylland, an 18-year-old Rashford was given his first-ever start for the Red Devils after Anthony Martial got injured in the warm-up. Not only that – he scored two goals in a 5-1 victory!

ICON!

Marcus has tirelessly campaigned against homelessness and child hunger in the UK and used his profile to raise awareness to drive change. He's also written a book to inspire children, called You Are A Champion, and been given an MBE by the Queen!

JUNE 2018

JUNE 2019

AUGUST 2020

JUNE 2021

TURN OVER FOR MORE!

RASH MAN TO THE RESCUE!

STAT ATTACK!

He's only 23, but Rashford has already clocked up some serious numbers for United in the Prem!

2015-16
GAMES 11   GOALS 5   ASSISTS 2

2016-17
GAMES 32   GOALS 5   ASSISTS 1

2017-18
GAMES 35   GOALS 7   ASSISTS 5

2018-19
GAMES 33   GOALS 10   ASSISTS 6

2019-20
GAMES 31   GOALS 17   ASSISTS 7

2020-21
GAMES 37   GOALS 11   ASSISTS 9

FIFA LEVEL UP!

76 ST — RASHFORD
90 PAC   79 DRI
73 SHO   31 DEF
66 PAS   65 PHY
BASIC

THEN FIFA 17

85 LM — RASHFORD
91 PAC   85 DRI
83 SHO   45 DEF
78 PAS   78 PHY

NOW FIFA 21

"I think Marcus is way ahead of where I was when I was 23. I was still trying to figure things out. He is already making changes and being a positive force in his community!" President Barack Obama

THREE LIONS LEADER!

After making his England debut in 2016, he's gone on to make 46 appearances in an England shirt, scoring 12 goals so far, but on 6 June 2021, Rash stepped out against Romania at Wembley as the skipper – a huge moment in his career!

7 EPIC THINGS MARCUS HAS ACHIEVED!

↘ **EXPERT PANEL AWARD WINNER AT BBC SPORTS PERSONALITY OF THE YEAR 2020**

↘ **TIME MAGAZINE TOP 100 MOST INFLUENTIAL PEOPLE**

↘ **2020 PFA MERIT AWARD WINNER**

↘ **UEFA EUROPA LEAGUE SQUAD OF THE SEASON 2019-20**

↘ **CAMPAIGNER OF THE YEAR AT THE 2020 GQ AWARDS**

↘ **GUARDIAN FOOTBALLER OF THE YEAR 2020**

↘ **RAISED MORE THAN £20m FOR THE CHARITY FARESHARE**

Keep up to date with all the latest footy news at bbc.co.uk/sport BBC SPORT

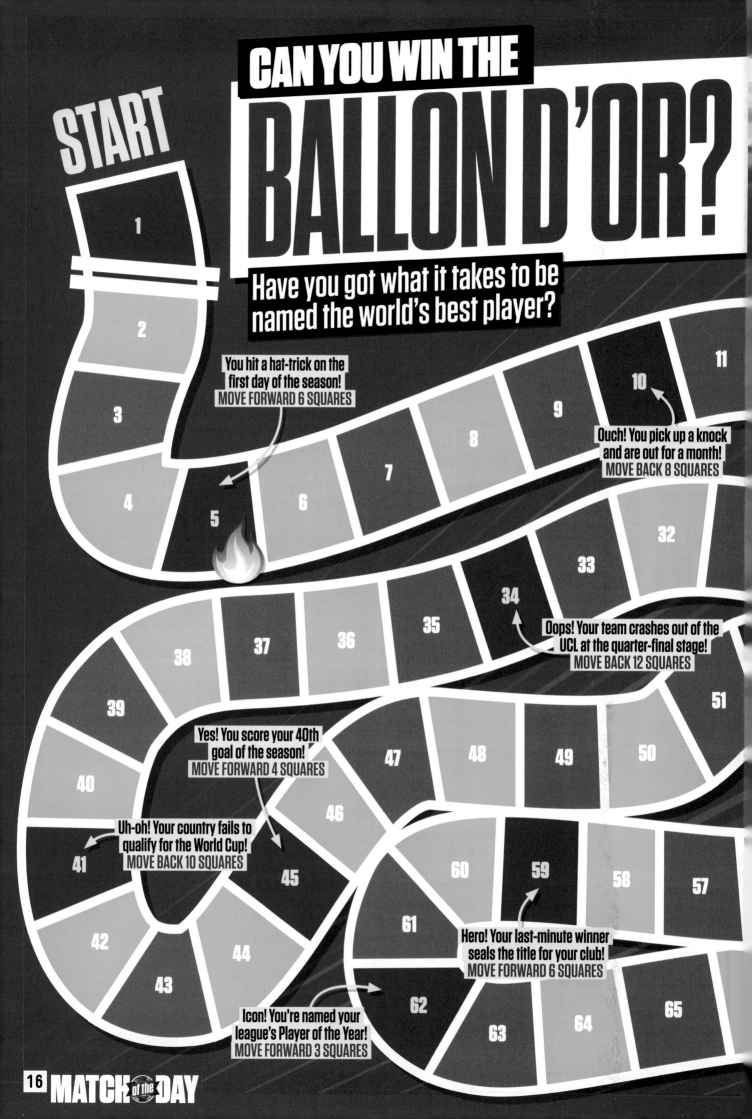

CAN YOU WIN THE BALLON D'OR?

Have you got what it takes to be named the world's best player?

START

1
2
3
4
5

You hit a hat-trick on the first day of the season!
MOVE FORWARD 6 SQUARES

6
7
8
9
10
11

Ouch! You pick up a knock and are out for a month!
MOVE BACK 8 SQUARES

32
33
34
35
36
37
38
39
40
41
42
43
44
45
46
47
48
49
50
51

Oops! Your team crashes out of the UCL at the quarter-final stage!
MOVE BACK 12 SQUARES

Yes! You score your 40th goal of the season!
MOVE FORWARD 4 SQUARES

Uh-oh! Your country fails to qualify for the World Cup!
MOVE BACK 10 SQUARES

57
58
59
60
61
62
63
64
65

Hero! Your last-minute winner seals the title for your club!
MOVE FORWARD 6 SQUARES

Icon! You're named your league's Player of the Year!
MOVE FORWARD 3 SQUARES

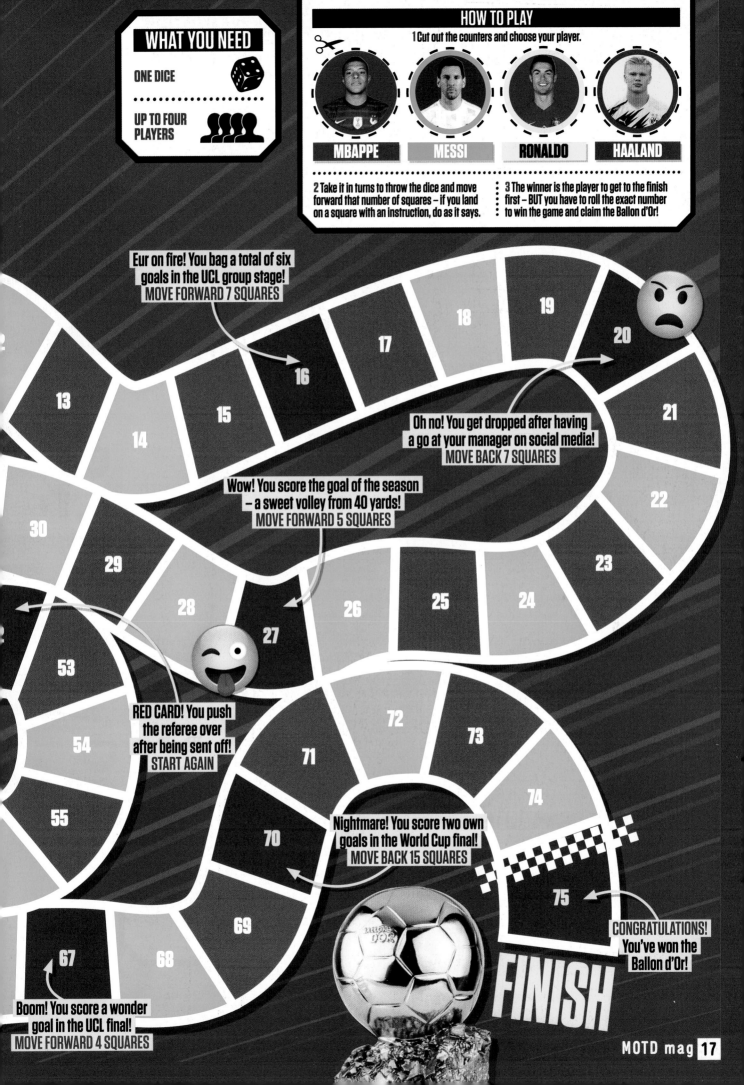

WHAT YOU NEED

ONE DICE

UP TO FOUR PLAYERS

HOW TO PLAY

1 Cut out the counters and choose your player.

MBAPPE **MESSI** **RONALDO** **HAALAND**

2 Take it in turns to throw the dice and move forward that number of squares – if you land on a square with an instruction, do as it says.

3 The winner is the player to get to the finish first – BUT you have to roll the exact number to win the game and claim the Ballon d'Or!

Eur on fire! You bag a total of six goals in the UCL group stage!
MOVE FORWARD 7 SQUARES

Oh no! You get dropped after having a go at your manager on social media!
MOVE BACK 7 SQUARES

Wow! You score the goal of the season – a sweet volley from 40 yards!
MOVE FORWARD 5 SQUARES

RED CARD! You push the referee over after being sent off!
START AGAIN

Nightmare! You score two own goals in the World Cup final!
MOVE BACK 15 SQUARES

CONGRATULATIONS! You've won the Ballon d'Or!

FINISH

Boom! You score a wonder goal in the UCL final!
MOVE FORWARD 4 SQUARES

13 14 15 16 17 18 19 20 21 22 23 24 25 26 27 28 29 30 53 54 55 67 68 69 70 71 72 73 74 75

STEVE BRUCE'S FANCY DRESS!

Give Brucey some new threads and some snacks to put a smile on his face!

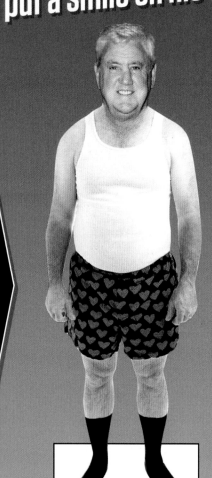

WHAT YOU NEED TO DO!

1 Get a parent or guardian to help you cut out Steve Bruce using a pair of scissors.

2 Next, you need to stick him onto a piece of cardboard so he stands up nice and straight.

3 Cut out the other items on this page and place them on to Brucey, folding the tabs around the body to keep them in place.

4 Tell him how mint he looks in his brand-new garms – he'll love that!

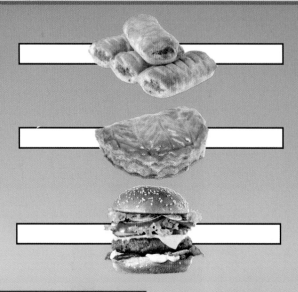

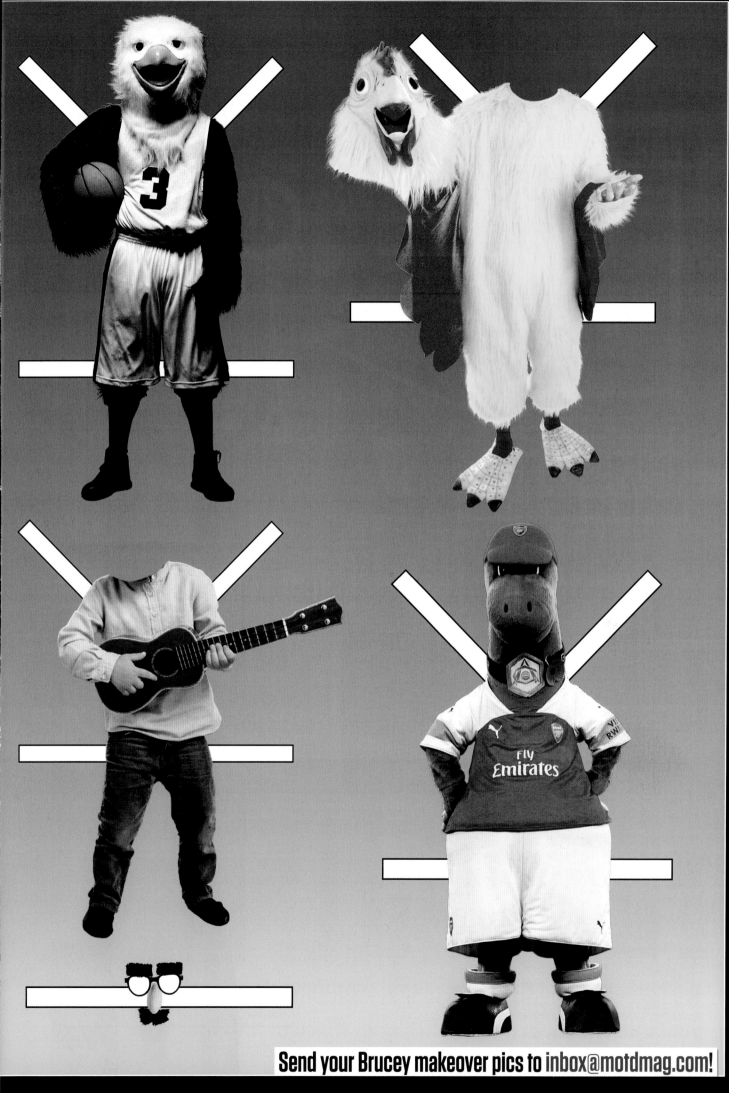

Send your Brucey makeover pics to inbox@motdmag.com!

THE BIG MAP OF FOOTBALL!

WETHERBY ROAD HARROGATE
SMALLEST STADIUM IN THE EFL, CAPACITY OF 5,000

OLD TRAFFORD MAN. UNITED
BIGGEST STADIUM IN THE PREM, CAPACITY OF 74,140

PRESTON
FIRST-EVER CHAMPIONS OF ENGLAND IN 1889

MAN. UNITED
MOST ENGLISH TITLE WINS, 20

MAN. CITY
CURRENT PREMIER LEAGUE CHAMPIONS

BIRTHPLACE OF WAYNE ROONEY
ENGLAND'S RECORD GOALSCORER
LIVERPOOL, 24 OCTOBER 1985

MILLENNIUM STADIUM
BIGGEST STADIUM IN WALES, CAPACITY OF 74,500

We take a look at the most iconic moments, biggest stadiums and best players from the world of football!

FIRST-EVER INTERNATIONAL
SCOTLAND 0-0 ENGLAND
GLASGOW, 30 NOVEMBER 1872

RANGERS
MOST SCOTTISH TITLE WINS, 55

CELTIC PARK CELTIC
BIGGEST STADIUM IN SCOTLAND, CAPACITY OF 60,411

BIRTHPLACE OF ALAN SHEARER
PREMIER LEAGUE RECORD GOALSCORER
NEWCASTLE, 13 AUGUST 1970

ENGLAND WIN THE WORLD CUP
WEMBLEY STADIUM, LONDON, 1966

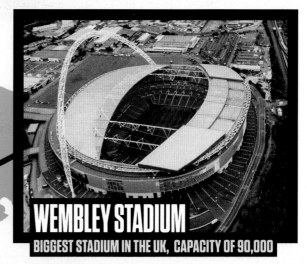

WEMBLEY STADIUM
BIGGEST STADIUM IN THE UK, CAPACITY OF 90,000

CHELSEA WOMEN
MOST WSL TITLE WINS, FOUR

ARSENAL
MOST FA CUP WINS, 14

THE BIG MAP OF FOOTBALL!

17-YEAR-OLD PELE BECOMES A SUPERSTAR
1958 WORLD CUP FINAL, ULLEVI STADIUM, SWEDEN

BARCELONA
BEST CLUB TEAM OF ALL TIME, 2008-12

REAL MADRID
MOST EUROPEAN CUP & CHAMPIONS LEAGUE WINS, 13

MARADONA'S HAND OF GOD GOAL v ENGLAND
1986 WORLD CUP, AZTECA STADIUM, MEXICO

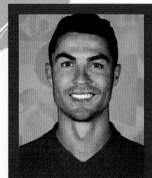

BIRTHPLACE OF CRISTIANO RONALDO
FUNCHAL, MADEIRA, PORTUGAL, 5 FEBRUARY 1985

HOME OF THE SUPERCLASICO WORLD'S BIGGEST DERBY
BUENOS AIRES, ARGENTINA, BOCA JUNIORS v RIVER PLATE

MIROSLAV KLOSE BECOMES WORLD CUP RECORD GOALSCORER
BRAZIL 1-7 GERMANY, 2014 WORLD CUP, BRAZIL

BIRTHPLACE OF LIONEL MESSI
ROSARIO, ARGENTINA, 24 JUNE 1987

BRAZIL
MOST WORLD CUP WINS, FIVE

JOHAN CRUYFF INVENTS THE CRUYFF TURN
1974 WORLD CUP, WESTFALENSTADION, GERMANY

GERMANY & SPAIN
**MOST EUROPEAN
CHAMPIONSHIP WINS, THREE**

ANTONIN PANENKA INVENTS
THE PANENKA PENALTY
**EURO 76, RED STAR STADIUM,
YUGOSLAVIA**

MARSEILLE
**FIRST WINNERS OF THE
CHAMPIONS LEAGUE, 1993**

MIRACLE OF ISTANBUL
**LIVERPOOL COME FROM 3-0 DOWN
TO BEAT AC MILAN IN 2005 UCL FINAL,
ATATURK STADIUM, TURKEY**

NOU CAMP BARCELONA
BIGGEST STADIUM IN EUROPE, CAPACITY OF 99,354

BIGGEST WIN IN AN INTERNATIONAL MATCH
AUSTRALIA 31-0 AMERICAN SAMOA, 2001

Classic SCHOOL 11!

A who's who of the players every team has!

GK
THE NON-GOALIE

RB
THE SURPRISE STAR

CB
THE MOANER

CB
THE TEACHER'S PET

LB
THE FUNNY ONE

CM
THE KNOW-IT-ALL

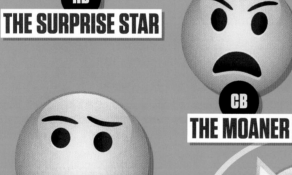

CAM
THE VIDEO CLIPPER

CM
THE BATTLER

FW
THE SPEED DEMON

ST
THE NEW BOOTS

FW
THE HOGGER

THE LINE-UP!

These ballers are in teams everywhere. You probably know one – or you might even *BE* one!

GK
THE NON-GOALIE

Everyone knows this classmate would rather be pinging cross-field balls around the pitch but the gaffer didn't care, threw them the gloves and they actually did quite well!

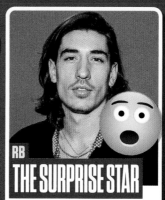

RB
THE SURPRISE STAR

This little gem is top of the class, goes to the library at lunchtime and attends drama after-school club. But they turned up to a training session and were one of the best players!

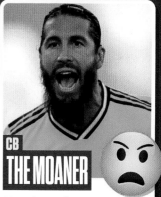

CB
THE MOANER

Watch out, because this foghorn would moan about getting wet in a swimming pool! If they're not having a go at the referee, they're asking the gaffer to make a sub. Zip it, will ya?!

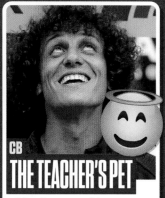

CB
THE TEACHER'S PET

This player could score nine own goals or get a silly red card, but they'd still be the first name on the teamsheet in the next game because they suck up to the gaffer so much!

LB
THE FUNNY ONE

It's mad, because this lefty is a low-key decent baller, but you wouldn't know it because they're too busy trying to make their mates laugh with dives, tricks and mad scorpion kicks!

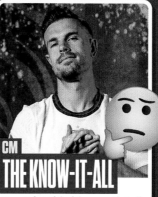

CM
THE KNOW-IT-ALL

Don't let this big mouth tell you what to do. Yeah, they might have played one game for Chelsea U-7s, but it doesn't mean they can boss you about or tell the gaffer when to make subs!

CM
THE BATTLER

This guy doesn't say a word, and they keep their head down in the changing room. They just lace up, hit the pitch and put their body on the line for the team every game!

CAM
THE VIDEO CLIPPER

Here's what to expect with this social-media star – they'll walk around doing nothing for 89 minutes, but net a late tap-in and post pics of the celebrations like they were the MVP!

FW
THE HOGGER

If this baller could take a throw-in to themselves, they would! Don't expect the ball back if you pass to them. They've got the skills, but their selfishness drives you absolutely mad!

LW
THE SPEED DEMON

Trust, if this player gets the ball near goal, it's hitting the science block! They've got zero tekkers and it's sometimes like their boots are on the wrong feet, but they've got absolute pace!

ST
THE NEW BOOTS

Puma Futures – got. Fresh Nike Mercurials – in the bag. Adidas Preds – on next day delivery. It really doesn't matter how well this player balls, they've got the very latest kicks!

DIEGO
MARADONA

ARGENTINA

THE ALTERNATIVE

A Z
OF FOOTBALL
IN 2021!

After a totally bonkers 2020-21 football season, get a load of MOTD mag's equally crazy guide!

B IS FOR...
BEN BRERETON DIAZ

NO-ONE HAD HEARD of Benjamin Anthony Brereton in Chile at the start of 2021 – but now he's a national hero! Brereton, born and raised in Stoke-on-Trent, currently plays for Blackburn. But because his mum was born in Chile, Brereton got a call-up to their Copa America squad and SCORED THE WINNING GOAL in his first start!

CHILE!

STOKE-ON-TRENT!

A IS FOR...
ADIOS, SERGIO

AFTER 16 SEASONS, 671 games, 101 goals, 26 red cards, five La Liga titles and four Champions League wins, Sergio Ramos waved adios to the Bernabeu earlier this year. He arrived at Real Madrid in 2005 as a highly rated, 19-year-old right-back, and he left for PSG as a highly decorated, 35-year-old legend!

C IS FOR...

CITY

WHAT A YEAR 2021 was for the Cities of English football. Man. CITY celebrated their third Premier League title in four years, Norwich CITY were crowned Championship champions and Hull CITY were League One champions. Only League Two champions Cheltenham TOWN stopped a city clean sweep!

HULL CITY!

MAN. CITY!

NORWICH CITY!

D IS FOR...
DRAGON STADIUM

THAT'S THE ENGLISH translation of the Estadio Do Dragao, in Porto, which hosted the Champions League final between Chelsea and Man. City in May. City were favourites, with Pep Guardiola looking for his first UCL title for a decade – but Chelsea won 1-0 thanks to a Kai Havertz strike!

E IS FOR...
EL LOCO

El Loco means 'mad man' in Spanish!

BORN AS WASHINGTON Sebastian Abreu Gallo, better known as Sebastian Abreu, but best of all known by his nickname El Loco, the 44-year-old Uruguayan striker finally hung up his boots earlier this year after a crazy 26-year career which saw him play for 31 different clubs in 11 different countries!

El Loco won 70 caps for Uruguay over 16 years!

F IS FOR...
FC AUGSBERG II

ON 1 JULY 2007, Augsberg appointed an unknown 34-year-old German coach as manager of their reserve team. Little did anyone know back then, just how much of an impact that young manager would have on English football in 2021. That man, Thomas Tuchel, went on to manage Mainz, Borussia Dortmund and PSG before arriving at Chelsea in January 2021 – and less than five months later, he'd already written his name into the club's history books!

It's your boy Tommy T before anyone knew who he was!

TUCHEL AT CHELSEA JANUARY TO JUNE 2021

Champions League winner!

March Manager of the Month!

11 clean sheets in 19 Prem games

OVERALL RECORD

P	W	D	L	F	A	WIN %
30	19	6	5	37	16	63.33

TURN OVER FOR MORE!

G IS FOR... GDANSK

TOURISTS FLOCK to this Polish coastal city every year – but one person who won't be back in a hurry is Man. United keeper David De Gea. His last visit was in May for the Europa League Final – and it didn't go well. United lost 11-10 on penalties – De Gea failed to save any AND missed the final penalty!

H IS FOR... HARRY KANE

ANOTHER YEAR, ANOTHER year of Harry Kane doing Harry Kane things. The England captain won this THIRD Premier League Golden Boot by scoring 23 goals from 35 matches. He also became the first player to win the Premier League Playmaker of the Season award in the same campaign after bagging 14 assists!

I IS FOR... IVAN BENJAMIN ELIJAH TONEY

KANE MAY HAVE won the Premier League Golden Boot, but there's another guy in the Premier League who scored more goals than him last season – and that's Brentford's Ivan Toney. Northampton-born Toney hit an impressive 31 goals as the Bees secured promotion to the Prem for the first time in their history. It's fair to say Toney is the best thing to come out of Northampton since Francis Crick, the fella who discovered DNA!

Toney was also League One top scorer the season before!

K IS FOR... KICKER-TORJAGERKANONE

IN ENGLAND, THE top goalscorer gets a Golden Boot, but in the Bundesliga they get a mad miniature cannon! The Torjagerkanone – which literally means 'scorer cannon' – is awarded by German sports magazine Kicker, and for 2020-21, unsurprisingly, it went to Robert Lewandowski. His 41 goals was a league record, and it was his fourth Bundesliga top scorer award in a row!

Lewa has hit 203 goals in 209 league games for Bayern!

J IS FOR...

"JUST BLOW THE FULL-TIME WHISTLE, REF!"

IF YOU'RE A Southampton fan, just go to the letter K. Because in February, just 16 months after losing 9-0 to Leicester, Saints travelled to Old Trafford and, oops – it happened again! Ralph Hasenhuttl's team were thumped 9-0 by a Man. United team who'd only scored nine goals in their previous eight games. Spare a thought for Saints midfielder James Ward-Prowse – he was the only Saints player on the pitch for all 18 goals in those two 9-0 defeats!

L IS FOR...

LIONEL ANDRES MESSI

THIS WAS THE year Leo finally got his hands on the first international trophy of his career, as Argentina won the Copa America. He was also top scorer and named player of the tournament. With Barcelona, he was La Liga top scorer for a record eighth time, he won the Copa Del Rey, he became Barca's record appearance holder and the first player to score 30-plus goals in 13 consecutive club seasons. GOAT!

M IS FOR...

MAPEI STADIUM

IT WAS AT this stadium in northern Italy that Inter Milan won their first Serie A title for 11 years – without even playing! The 21,000-capacity ground is the home of Sassuolo, and it was their 1-1 draw with Inter's title rivals Atalanta in May that saw the Milan giants crowned Italian champions for the 19th time!

TURN OVER FOR MORE!

N IS FOR...
NINETY PLUS FIVE

LIVERPOOL ARE DRAWING 1-1 with West Brom in the fifth minute of injury time back in May, their hopes of a Champions League spot are crumbling. But then the Reds force a corner, Trent Alexander-Arnold swings it in and Liverpool keeper Alisson Becker rises highest to score the winner. Absolute scenes!

O IS FOR...
ORJANS VALL

ROY HODGSON WAS handed his very first managerial role in 1976 when he became boss of Swedish club Halmstads. He became a legend at Orjans Vall, the club's stadium, after winning the title in his very first season. This summer, Roy stepped down as Crystal Palace boss, ending a career which saw him manage 16 teams in eight countries, including five national team jobs!

ORJANS VALL STADIUM!

P IS FOR...
PORTUGUESE KING OF ENGLAND

Bruno Fernandes has taken to life at Old Trafford like a little Portuguese duck to water. He finished last season with 28 goals in all comps – the most EVER in a single season by a Premier League midfielder. He also bagged 17 assists and claimed his crown as spot-kick king after scoring a staggering 13 pens in 2020-21!

Only Kane and Salah scored more Prem goals than Bruno last season!

R IS FOR...

RONALDO, CRISTIANO

C'MON, HE'S 36 now. He should be winding down, spending Sunday afternoons at the garden centre and watching Coronation Street with a nice cup of cocoa. But no, not CR7. In 2021, he won the Serie A Golden Boot, becoming the only player to finish as top scorer in Italy, England and Spain. He also became the top scorer in Euros history and took his career total to almost 800 goals!

Ron was also top scorer at Euro 2020!

THE QUEEN!

Q IS FOR...

QUEEN'S BIRTHDAY BOYS

ENGLAND PAIR RAHEEM Sterling and Jordan Henderson got a nice present from the Queen back in June. They were both awarded MBEs in the Queen's Birthday Honours List, which recognises people for their achievements. Raheem got his for his campaigning against racial injustice, while Henderson was rewarded for services to football and charity, especially during the Covid pandemic!

S IS FOR...

STOCKPORT

STOCKPORT IS A town in Greater Manchester, seven miles south-east of Manchester city centre. In the 16th Century it was famous for making rope, in the 18th Century it was famous for its silk factory, and in the 19th Century it was famous for making hats. But from now on, it'll be known as the birthplace of 2021's breakout star – Philip Walter Foden!

Phil was PFA Young Player of the Year for 2020-21!

STOCKPORT!

TURN OVER FOR MORE!

Remy played for QPR, Chelsea, Newcastle and Crystal Palace!

T IS FOR...

TURKISH BLAST FROM THE PAST

Last season, you couldn't check the Turkish results without familiar names staring back at you – ex-Prem attackers you assumed had retired YEARS AGO! These are the guys we're talking about...

ARE YOU STILL PLAYING? Mame Biram Diouf, Enner Valencia, Hugo Rodallega, Max Gradel, Fabio Borini, Loic Remy, Ryan Babel, Demba Ba, Papiss Cisse, Lukas Podolski, Gabriel Obertan and Arouna Kone!

U IS FOR... UCL TOP SCORER!

ERLING HAALAND doesn't break records, he smashes them into smithereens! His ten goals in last season's UCL not only won him the competition's golden boot, it also took him to 20 UCL goals in just 14 games – seeing him become the quickest EVER to reach that figure. He bagged 41 goals in all competitions last season, taking his total to 85 goals in his last 81 games!

BELLINGHAM & SANCHO!

V IS FOR...

VALLADOLID

THIS CITY IN north-west Spain was the unlikely scene of a huge title party back in May. It was the final day of the La Liga season and Atletico Madrid, needing a win to pip city rivals Real to the Spanish title, came from behind to secure a 2-1 victory. It saw Diego Simeone's side crowned Spanish champions for the first time in seven years!

W IS FOR...

WESTFALENSTADION

ONE OF THE most atmospheric stadiums in world football is home to German giants Borussia Dortmund – and the 2020-21 season saw it become the stage for two young super-talented English ballers. You know all about Jude Bellingham and Jadon Sancho – now it's home to just Jude after Jadon's Man. United move!

YILMAZ, BURAK

AT THE START of 2021, only a fool would have bet against PSG becoming French champions for the eighth time in nine years. But it seems no-one told Lille or their big striker Burak Yilmaz. The 36-year-old Turkish striker was the unlikely hero, scoring 16 goals as Lille pipped PSG to the Ligue 1 title by one point!

This was Lille's first title for ten years!

X IS FOR... XAVI

NOT HAPPY WITH simply being the best Spanish midfielder of all time, Xavi is now proving to be just as influential in the dug-out as boss of Al Sadd in Qatar. The Barcelona legend led his team to a record 15th league title this year – and they did it without losing a single game! Don't be surprised if you see him back at Barca as boss some time soon!

Z IS FOR... ZOOM CALLS

THE DAYS OF packed press conferences or chatting to players in the training ground canteen have become a thing of the past thanks to Covid – boooo! Now, interviews are done over Zoom – just like Chelsea's Magdalena Eriksson, a 2021 WSL title winner, is doing here! Just don't forget to unmute, Mags!

Eriksson won the WSL with Chelsea in 2020-21!

Watch Prem highlights on MOTD, Saturday evenings, on BBC One

WOMEN'S FOOTBALL
DREAM TEAM!

MOTD mag has searched the globe to compile this, the strongest team of women's superstars in the game today!

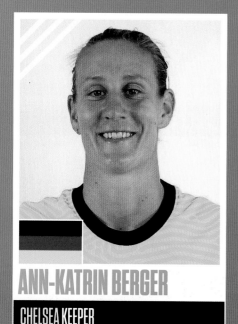

ANN-KATRIN BERGER
CHELSEA KEEPER

CRYSTAL DUNN
PORTLAND THORNS LEFT-BACK

LEAH WILLIAMSON
ARSENAL CENTRE-BACK

WENDIE RENARD
LYON CENTRE-BACK

LUCY BRONZE
MAN. CITY RIGHT-BACK

SAM MEWIS
NORTH CAROLINA COURAGE MIDFIELDER

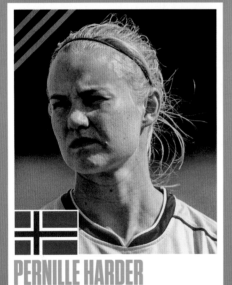

PERNILLE HARDER
CHELSEA MIDFIELDER

AMEL MAJRI
LYON WINGER

CAROLINE GRAHAM HANSEN
BARCELONA WINGER

SAM KERR
CHELSEA STRIKER

VIVIANNE MIEDEMA
ARSENAL STRIKER

BERGER

WILLIAMSON RENARD

BRONZE   DUNN

MEWIS → HARDER

HANSEN   MAJRI

KERR   MIEDEMA

WHO'S BEATING THIS?

MATCH **of the DAY**
magazine

P A U L   G A S C O I G N E

GAZZA

E N G L A N D

57 caps / 10 goals / Born Gateshead 1967 / Midfielder / joker / genius

YOUR BIG WINNERS OF 2022!

Our magical word grids below will help you predict next year's heroes and champions!

GRID 1
The first club you see will be your 2021-22 Premier League title winner!

```
M A H N E T T O T M
N O R W I C H I U A
S L W O L V E S A N
C H E L S E A B R U
Z T R A R Q I L S N
M A N C I T Y R E I
B U R N L E Y S N T
E V E R T O N F A E
L I V E R P O O L D
L E E D S F M O L P
```

GRID 2
The first surname you see will be your 2021-22 Player of the Year winner!

```
H M J F M J G W I Q
J O E L I N T O N Z
T O N E Y Y P O G V
L I N G A R D D S A
F E R N A N D E S N
D U N K A N T E O D
D E B R U Y N E N I
M I L N E R E Z E J
G R E A L I S H F K
K A N E X F O D E N
```

GRID 3
The first surname you see is your 2021-22 Prem Golden Boot winner!

```
D L H V S W I V D V
S N I A X U T D Q R
A N L P V A R D Y A
L A I P I O D K M S
A V U K F H H A A H
H I Q M T V P N N F
W A T K I N S E E O
T B A M F O R D Y R
W E R N E R Z P B D
G N S T E R L I N G
```

GRID 4
The first country you see is your 2022 World Cup winner!

```
F B I E G Q R U B A
V E T I N A H L R R
F L A O T T I A A G
R G L A Y A L U Z E
A I Y W A R Y A I N
N U S R D J Z L L T
C M B S P A I N A I
E V L A G U T R O N
P O R T U G A L S A
L T O E N G L A N D
```

MY WINNERS OF 2022!

PREMIER LEAGUE ....

PLAYER OF THE YEAR ....

GOLDEN BOOT ....

2022 WORLD CUP ....

TEKK HEROES

- Who is the corner kick king?
- Who hits the sweetest volleys?
- Which baller makes scoring penalties look easy?

From stamina to speed and loads more, MOTD mag presents the best of the best tekknicians!

ERS
S!

ULTIMATE
BALLERS ALERT!
THESE PLAYERS
ARE TOTALLY OFF
THE SCALE!

TURN OVER FOR MORE!

TOUCH

LIONEL MESSI BARCELONA

If this picture of Leo catching the ball above his head on the end of his toe doesn't convince you he's got the best control in world footy, then maybe his team-mates' amazed faces will. And if that doesn't, we can't help you!

FREE-KICKS

LIONEL MESSI BARCELONA

Don't ever give away a foul on the edge of the box when Leo is knocking about. Why? Well, because he'll place the ball down, take three steps back and two to the right, then take a light jog up to it, before whipping it up and over the wall into the top bins!

STAMINA

N'GOLO KANTE
CHELSEA

If every baller in the world lined up for the London Marathon, there would only be one winner – N'Golo. The France midfielder covers every inch of the pitch and doesn't stop until the final whistle blows. Even then, he probably does extra work!

PENALTIES

CRISTIANO RONALDO JUVENTUS

When the referee points to the penalty spot, there is only player you want to be standing over the kick – and that is C-Ron. By the end of Euro 2020, the Portugal penalty king had netted 139 in his career, compared to his GOAT rival Lionel Messi, who has only scored 101!

VOLLEYS

LUIS SUAREZ
ATLETICO MADRID

He did it for Liverpool and Barcelona, and now he's doing it for Atletico Madrid. Luis can track the flight of a ball with razor-sharp vision, judge its arrival and connect like he's trying to blast the ball into 1,000 pieces. If it's flying through the air, Suarez is gonna pounce on it!

TURN OVER FOR MORE!

SHOT-STOPPING

JAN OBLAK ATLETICO MADRID

Sometimes it seems like the Atletico Madrid No.1 has eight arms. Oblak's reflexes and shot-stopping skills are an absolute madness – anything that comes his way, he bats it away like he's protecting a huge pot of gold behind him!

CORNERS

TRENT ALEXANDER-ARNOLD LIVERPOOL

From a dead-ball situation, Trent has all the angles and tek in his locker to deliver the perfect set piece. Low driller? No problem. Hanging drifter? Coming right up. Pure whippage? Here we go. Liverpool's versatile gem is the ultimate corner king!

CROSSING

KEVIN DE BRUYNE MAN. CITY

KDB's power control on his crossing is what sets him apart from the rest. The weight he puts on the connection is always absolutely elite, making it easy for oncoming attackers to finish the chance. He's one of the world's top assisters, and this is a major reason why!

SKILLS

NEYMAR PSG

Most five-star skillers have loads of tricks in their locker but only try them in training. The cool thing about street baller Ney is that he's not afraid to try them in real matches. We rate his confidence very highly!

DRIBBLING

LIONEL MESSI BARCELONA

Imagine what it would be like to watch ten outfield players running around trying to catch an opposition player who has the ball glued to his foot. Pah! Guess what? You don't have to imagine – just watch the main man Messi do his bits. No-one can ever get the thing off him!

TURN OVER FOR MORE!

PASSING

THIAGO ALCANTARA LIVERPOOL

When you've come up through the Barcelona academy, it's no surprise that possession-based football gives you life. Thiago knows when to keep it simple, when to break defensive lines with sick through balls and when to switch the play to create overloads. He's a pass master!

TACKLES

N'GOLO KANTE CHELSEA

The best thing about Kante's tackling tekkers is that no-one ever sees it coming! He nips around with his invisibility jacket on, then pops up out of nowhere to steal the ball. He's an absolute nightmare for midfielders trying to break forward and start attacks!

HEADERS

VIRGIL VAN DIJK
LIVERPOOL

Is it a bird? Is it a plane? Nope, it's Virgil van Dijk rocketing through the air to connect with yet another bulldozing header. The Dutch destroyer leaps higher and connects with more power than anyone else, and he wins way more aerial battles than he loses. VVD is a heading hero!

VISION

KEVIN DE BRUYNE
MAN. CITY

We swear sometimes KDB is a robot. If he's not, can someone explain how he sees passes that not even the TV cameraman can keep up with? He's got the perfect picture of how football should be played in his head and, guess what, he makes it happen!

SPEED

KYLIAN MBAPPE PSG

Yep, that's right – PSG speed machine Mbappe is so fast that not even the photographer could quite capture him in full motion for this pitcture. He once recorded a six-yard speed of 22.4mph against Marseille in February 2021. It's crazy, but he's even quicker WITH the ball!

LILLE
LIGUE 1 CHAMPIONS

202

LEA
WIN

RANGERS SCOTTISH
PREMIERSHIP CHAMPIONS

FOREVER IN MY HEART
ELESIKA IK AMUSI
AN BO OLI
I LOVE YOU AND I MISS YOU

INTER MILAN
SERIE A CHAMPIONS

ATLETICO MADRID
LA LIGA CHAMPIONS

BAYERN MUNICH
BUNDESLIGA CHAMPIONS

-21
GUE
IERS

SHIP
0/2

WINNER

UEFA EL

THE BEST EUROS EVER

Euro 2020 produced some seriously magical moments. Here's a look through the lens at some of the highlights!

EURO 2020

ITALY

IN PICTURES!

TURN OVER FOR MORE!

FLYING HIGH!
A Greenpeace protestor parachuted onto the pitch before France's group-stage clash with Germany!

CZECH MATE!
The Netherlands were dumped out by the Czech Republic – just look what it meant to the players!

ITALIAN PASSION!
Watching Italy belt out their national anthem was as impressive as the football they played!

KANE SINKS GERMANY!

Kyle Walker jumps for joy after Harry Kane netted the second in England's 2-0 win over Germany!

TOTAL SCENES!

How buzzing were the Three Lions with Raheem Sterling's opener v Germany? See for yourselves!

TURN OVER FOR MORE!

ALL OF THE LIGHTS!
Opening ceremonies don't come much bigger than what we saw in Rome at the Italy v Turkey game!

GREAT DANES!
The Denmark squad celebrate with their fans after dramatically qualifying for the knockout rounds!

TANGERINE DREAM!
The Netherlands' summer got off to a flying start, thanks to Georginio Wijnaldum's goal against Ukraine!

NOOOOOOOO!
When Patrik Schick let fly from the halfway line, Scotland keeper David Marshall was left scrambling!

HUNGARY FOR MORE!
The Hungarians were pure vibes after their shock 1-1 draw with the reigning World Cup champs France!

TURN OVER FOR MORE!

WE LOVE YOU, CHRISTIAN!
When Romelu Lukaku scored v Russia, he had a special message for Inter Milan pal Christian Eriksen!

GOAT TALK!
After France played Portugal, one ledge, Cristiano Ronaldo, caught up with a future king, Kylian Mbappe!

SAME TEK, DIFFERENT DAY!
Cristiano Ronaldo scored five at Euro 2020 – the first of those from the penalty spot against Hungary!

GROUP CHAT!
Before Belgium's group game against Finland, they huddled up and, well, it looked kinda sick!

MATCH of the DAY magazine

XAVI

SPAIN

133 caps / 13 goals

Tiki-taka king

767 games for Barcelona

THE COUNTRY QUIZ!

Can you tell us where the clubs below come from?

HOW DID YOU DO?
TURN TO p92 FOR THE ANSWERS!

1

FC LORIENT
1926

A France ☐
B England ☐
C China ☐

2

GO AHEAD EAGLES
DEVENTER

A USA ☐
B South Africa ☐
C Netherlands ☐

3

ПАРТИЗАН PARTIZAN FUDBALSKI KLUB

A Bosnia ☐
B Croatia ☐
C Serbia ☐

4

LEVANTE U.D.

A France ☐
B Spain ☐
C Portugal ☐

5

CLUB INTERNACIONAL DE FÚTBOL
MIAMI
MMXX

A Mexico ☐
B USA ☐
C Brazil ☐

6

BRISBANE ROAR FC

A Scotland ☐
B Australia ☐
C Canada ☐

7

IFK NORRKÖPING

A Denmark ☐
B Norway ☐
C Sweden ☐

8

BSC YOUNG BOYS
YB
1898

A Austria ☐
B Switzerland ☐
C Belgium ☐

9

1.FC KÖLN

A Germany ☐
B Czech Republic ☐
C Poland ☐

30
YEARS OF THE
PREMIER

1992

MOTD mag celebrates three decades

LEAGUE!

2022

of the greatest league in the world!

TURN OVER FOR MORE!

HOW IT STARTED!

LIFE IN 1992!

» It's before the internet was even a thing
» It's the year before Harry Kane was born
» It's the year English football was transformed forever

THE FINAL TABLE FROM THE FIRST SEASON OF THE PREMIER LEAGUE, 1992-93!

	TEAM	P	W	D	L	F	A	Pts
1	Man. United	42	24	12	6	67	31	84
2	Aston Villa	42	21	11	10	57	40	74
3	Norwich	42	21	9	12	61	65	72
4	Blackburn	42	20	11	11	68	46	71
5	QPR	42	17	12	13	63	55	63
6	Liverpool	42	16	11	15	62	55	59
7	Sheffield Wednesday	42	15	14	13	55	51	59
8	Tottenham	42	16	11	15	60	66	59
9	Man. City	42	15	12	15	56	51	57
10	Arsenal	42	15	11	16	40	38	56
11	Chelsea	42	14	14	14	51	54	56
12	Wimbledon	42	14	12	16	56	55	54
13	Everton	42	15	8	19	53	55	53
14	Sheffield United	42	14	10	18	54	53	52
15	Coventry	42	13	13	16	52	57	52
16	Ipswich	42	12	16	14	50	55	52
17	Leeds	42	12	15	15	57	62	51
18	Southampton	42	13	11	18	54	61	50
19	Oldham	42	13	10	19	63	74	49
20	Crystal Palace	42	11	16	15	48	61	49
21	Middlesbrough	42	11	11	20	54	75	44
22	Nottingham Forest	42	10	10	22	41	62	40

THE CHANGING NAME OF THE PREM!

1992-93
FA PREMIER LEAGUE

1993-2001
FA CARLING PREMIERSHIP

2001-04
FA BARCLAYCARD PREMIERSHIP

2004-07
FA BARCLAYS PREMIERSHIP

2007-16
BARCLAYS PREMIER LEAGUE

2016 TO PRESENT
PREMIER LEAGUE

THE FIRST WINNERS!
Man. United, inspired by Eric Cantona, were the first champions of the Premier League era – it was their first league title for 26 years!

THE TOP SCORER!
Teddy Sheringham, who joined Tottenham from Nottingham Forest at the start of the 1992-93 season, won the first Golden Boot!

THE RECORD SIGNING!
MOTD pundit Alan Shearer was a highly rated 21-year-old striker who'd just joined Blackburn from Southampton for a record fee of £3.3m!

THE FAMILIAR FACE!
England manager Gareth Southgate was a 22-year-old centre-back back then – but he was already captain of Crystal Palace!

PREMIER LEAGUE CHAMPIONS!

These are the clubs that have finished top of the table since the Prem kicked off way back in 1992!

1992–93 MAN. UNITED

1993–94 MAN. UNITED

1994–95 BLACKBURN

1995–96 MAN. UNITED

1996–97 MAN. UNITED

1997–98 ARSENAL

1998–99 MAN. UNITED

1999–2000 MAN. UNITED

2000–01 MAN. UNITED

2001–02 ARSENAL

2002–03 MAN. UNITED

2003–04 ARSENAL

2004–05 CHELSEA

2005–06 CHELSEA

2006–07 MAN. UNITED

2007–08 MAN. UNITED

2008–09 MAN. UNITED

2009–10 CHELSEA

2010–11 MAN. UNITED

2011–12 MAN. CITY

2012–13 MAN. UNITED

2013–14 MAN. CITY

2014–15 CHELSEA

2015–16 LEICESTER

2016–17 CHELSEA

2017–18 MAN. CITY

2018–19 MAN. CITY

2019–20 LIVERPOOL

2020–21 MAN. CITY

THE SUPER SEVEN!

MAN. UNITED 13 PREM TITLES

CHELSEA 5 PREM TITLES

MAN. CITY 5 PREM TITLES

ARSENAL 3 PREM TITLES

BLACKBURN 1 PREM TITLE

LEICESTER 1 PREM TITLE

LIVERPOOL 1 PREM TITLE

TURN OVER FOR MORE!

PREMIER LEAGUE **ICONS!**

Thousands of players have graced the Premier League over the past three decades – but here is our all-time top ten!

10 SERGIO AGUERO

MAN. CITY 2011-21

Position	Striker
Country	Argentina
Prem seasons	10
Prem titles	5
Prem games/goals	275/184

Sergio will always be known for his dramatic title winner back in 2012 – City's first for 44 years – but it's his world-class goalscoring record over ten years that earns him a place in our top ten!

9 RYAN GIGGS

MAN. UNITED 1990-2014

Position	Winger
Country	Wales
Prem seasons	22
Prem titles	13
Prem games/goals	632/109

In terms of numbers, no-one comes close to the Man. United legend. He clocked up more than 1,000 games for club and country over 23 years, won 34 trophies and made a record 162 assists!

8 ROY KEANE

NOTTINGHAM FOREST & MAN. UNITED 1992-2005

Position	Midfielder
Country	Republic Of Ireland
Prem seasons	14
Prem titles	7
Prem games/goals	366/39

Tough-tackling Keano was the inspirational captain during Man. United's dominance of the 1990s. His never-say-die attitude, ball-winning and reading of the game make him a genuine Prem legend!

7 FRANK LAMPARD

WEST HAM, CHELSEA & MAN. CITY 1996-2015

Position	Midfielder
Country	England
Prem seasons	20
Prem titles	3
Prem games/goals	609/177

In 13 years at Chelsea, Lamps won the title three times and became the club's all-time top scorer. He also netted more goals than any other midfielder in Prem history!

6 PAUL SCHOLES

MAN. UNITED 1993-2013

Position	Midfielder
Country	England
Prem seasons	19
Prem titles	11
Prem games/goals	499/107

Scholesy evolved from a dynamic goal-scoring midfielder into a deep-lying playmaker – and was elite at both. The Prem's best-ever passer won 25 trophies, including two UCL wins!

5 WAYNE ROONEY

EVERTON & MAN. UNITED 2002-18

Position	Striker
Country	England
Prem seasons	16
Prem titles	5
Prem games/goals	491/208

Wazza burst onto the scene as a 16-year-old and went on to become Man. United's and England's record goalscorer. He could play as a No.9 or a No.10, score, create and produced moments of magic!

4 STEVEN GERRARD

LIVERPOOL 1998-2015

Position	Midfielder
Country	England
Prem seasons	17
Prem titles	0
Prem games/goals	504/120

No-one could grab a game by the scruff of its neck like this guy. His box-to-box running, his ferocious tackling, his cross-field balls and thunder-bolt shooting make him the Prem's best-ever midfielder!

3 ALAN SHEARER

BLACKBURN & NEWCASTLE 1992-2006

Position	Striker
Country	England
Prem seasons	14
Prem titles	1
Prem games/goals	441/260

The Premier League's record goalscorer was your classic No.9 – strong, powerful in the air and deadly in the box. But the three-time Golden Boot winner was most famous for his absolute cannon of a right foot!

2 CRISTIANO RONALDO

MAN. UNITED 2003–09

Position	Winger
Country	Portugal
Prem seasons	6
Prem titles	3
Prem games/goals	196/84

He arrived as a rapid, skilful, lightweight winger – and turned into an unstoppable match-winning machine. He left for Real Madrid before his peak – but the Prem still saw some phenomenal displays!

1 THIERRY HENRY

ARSENAL 1999-2007 & 2012

Position	Forward
Country	France
Prem seasons	9
Prem titles	2
Prem games/goals	258/175

This devastating attacker terrorised the Prem with pace, swagger and ice-cold finishing. Arsenal's all-time top scorer won the Golden Boot four times and set a record for the most assists in a season!

PREMIER LEAGUE DREAM TEAMS

1990s

PETER SCHMEICHEL

GARY NEVILLE — STEVE BRUCE — TONY ADAMS — DENNIS IRWIN

DAVID BECKHAM — ROY KEANE — PATRICK VIEIRA — RYAN GIGGS

ALAN SHEARER — ERIC CANTONA

2000s

PETR CECH

GARY NEVILLE — RIO FERDINAND — JOHN TERRY — ASHLEY COLE

FRANK LAMPARD — PAUL SCHOLES — STEVEN GERRARD

CRISTIANO RONALDO — WAYNE ROONEY — THIERRY HENRY

2010s

DAVID DE GEA

KYLE WALKER — VIRGIL VAN DIJK — VINCENT KOMPANY — LEIGHTON BAINES

N'GOLO KANTE

KEVIN DE BRUYNE — DAVID SILVA

MOHAMED SALAH — SERGIO AGUERO — EDEN HAZARD

TURN OVER FOR MORE!

PREMIER LEAGUE GOAL KINGS!

TOP 10 ALL-TIME RECORD GOALSCORERS

1 1992-2006 **ALAN SHEARER**
BLACKBURN, NEWCASTLE  **260** GOALS

2 2002-18 **WAYNE ROONEY**
EVERTON, MAN. UNITED **208** GOALS

3 1993-2008 **ANDY COLE**
NEWCASTLE, MAN. UNITED, BLACKBURN, FULHAM, MAN. CITY, PORTSMOUTH **187** GOALS

4 2011-21 **SERGIO AGUERO**
MAN. CITY **184** GOALS

5 1996-2015 **FRANK LAMPARD**
WEST HAM, CHELSEA, MAN. CITY **177** GOALS

6 1999-2012 **THIERRY HENRY**
ARSENAL **175** GOALS

7 2012-present **HARRY KANE**
TOTTENHAM **166** GOALS

8 1993-2008 **ROBBIE FOWLER**
LIVERPOOL, LEEDS, MAN. CITY **163** GOALS

9 2001-18 **JERMAIN DEFOE**
WEST HAM, TOTTENHAM, PORTSMOUTH, SUNDERLAND, BOURNEMOUTH **162** GOALS

10 1997-2013 **MICHAEL OWEN**
LIVERPOOL, NEWCASTLE, MAN. UNITED, STOKE **150** GOALS

BIG AL – THE MAN TO BEAT!

ALAN SHEARER holds a whole host of Prem goal records...
• He was the first player to score 200 Premier League goals
• He is the only player to score 100 goals for two different clubs
• He scored the most Prem pens – 56
• He scored the most goals from inside the penalty box – 227

THE ARGENTINIAN ASSASSIN!

SERGIO AGUERO, who spent ten years at Man. City before leaving for Barcelona in June, has scored the most goals for a single Premier League club. He is also the highest-scoring foreign player in Premier League history and also holds the record for most Premier League hat-tricks with 12!

THE THREE LIONS LEGEND!

HARRY KANE holds the record for the most Prem goals scored in a calendar year, after he bagged an impressive 39 for Tottenham in 2017. Also, no-one in the Premier League's 30-year history has a better strike rate than Kane – the England striker averages a goal every 1.47 games!

MOST GOALS IN A SEASON!

34 GOALS
ANDY COLE
Newcastle
1993-94
(42 matches)

34 GOALS
ALAN SHEARER
Blackburn
1994-95
(42 matches)

32 GOALS
MOHAMED SALAH
Liverpool
2017-18
(38 matches)

At the end of the 1994–95 season, the league was reduced from 22 teams to 20, resulting in four fewer matches for each club!

MOST GOALS IN A MATCH!

Five players have scored FIVE goals in a match in the history of the Premier League – they are...

ANDY COLE Man. United v Ipswich, 1994-95
ALAN SHEARER Newcastle v Sheffield Wed., 1999-2000
JERMAIN DEFOE Tottenham v Wigan, 2009-10
DIMITAR BERBATOV Man. United v Blackburn, 2010-11
SERGIO AGUERO Man. City v Newcastle, 2015-16

Watch Prem highlights on MOTD, Saturday evenings, on BBC One

MATCH of the DAY magazine

Ruud
Gullit

HAARLEM

FEYENOORD

PSV EINDHOVEN

AC MILAN

SAMPDORIA

CHELSEA

Netherlands / 66 caps / 17 goals / Born Amsterdam 1962

A YEAR IN FOOTBALL!

How much can you remember about 2021? Let's find out...

HOW DID YOU DO? TURN TO p92 FOR THE ANSWERS!

1 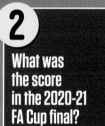 Who was named PFA Player of the Year last season?

A Kevin De Bruyne ☐
B Ruben Dias ☐
C Harry Kane ☐

2  What was the score in the 2020-21 FA Cup final?

A Chelsea 0-1 Leicester ☐
B Chelsea 1-0 Leicester ☐
C Chelsea 1-2 Leicester ☐

3  Which club beat Man. United in the Europa League final last season?

A Sevilla ☐
B Valencia ☐
C Villarreal ☐

4  Which Liverpool player was in the 2020-21 PFA Team of the Year?

A Alisson Becker ☐
B Andrew Robertson ☐
C Mohamed Salah ☐

5 Who scored the winning goal in the 2021 Champions League final back in May?

A Timo Werner ☐
B Kai Havertz ☐
C Antonio Rudiger ☐

6  Who was top scorer in La Liga last season?

A Karim Benzema ☐
B Lionel Messi ☐
C Luis Suarez ☐

7 Which European club appointed Jose Mourinho as their boss in May?

A Porto ☐
B Roma ☐
C Sevilla ☐

8 Who didn't take a penalty for England in the Euro 2020 final?

A Jordan Henderson ☐
B Harry Kane ☐
C Harry Maguire ☐

9  Who finished top scorer in Serie A last season?

A Ciro Immobile ☐
B Romelu Lukaku ☐
C Cristiano Ronaldo ☐

DAVOR SUKER

CROATIA

69 caps / 45 goals/ World Cup Golden Boot winner, 1998
Osijek / Dinamo Zagreb / Sevilla / Real Madrid / Arsenal / West Ham / 1860 Munich

GUESS WHO!

Can you name these Prem ballers from their profiles?

HOW DID YOU DO? TURN TO p92 FOR THE ANSWERS!

PLAYER 1

NAME ....

BORN		Bath, England
DATE OF BIRTH		13 March 1993 (age 28)

YEARS	CLUB	GAMES/GOALS
2011-12	Yate	
2012	Chippenham	13/0
2012-15	Ipswich	63/1
2015-19	Bournemouth	23/0
2019	Aston Villa (loan)	18/2
2019-	Aston Villa	73/4

PLAYER 2

NAME ....

BORN		Sheffield, England
DATE OF BIRTH		16 March 1997 (age 24)

YEARS	CLUB	GAMES/GOALS
2014-16	Sheffield United	12/0
2014-15	Stalybridge (loan)	5/6
2015-16	Northampton (loan)	26/8
2016-	Everton	173/53

PLAYER 3

NAME ....

BORN		Leicester, England
DATE OF BIRTH		13 July 1996 (age 25)

YEARS	CLUB	GAMES/GOALS
2012-13	Oadby	33/5
2013-14	Ilkeston	49/10
2014-16	Sheffield United	55/15
2016-19	Birmingham	123/38
2019-	Southampton	77/13

PLAYER 4

NAME ....

BORN		Porto, Portugal
DATE OF BIRTH		4 December 1996 (age 24)

YEARS	CLUB	GAMES/GOALS
2014-16	Pacos De Ferreira	45/15
2016-18	Atletico Madrid	0/0
2016-17	Porto (loan)	37/9
2017-18	Wolves (loan)	46/18
2018-20	Wolves	85/26
2020-	Liverpool	30/13

PLAYER 5

NAME ....

BORN		Berlin, Germany
DATE OF BIRTH		3 March 1993 (age 28)

YEARS	CLUB	GAMES/GOALS
2011-12	Stuttgart II	22/3
2012-16	Stuttgart	80/2
2015-16	Roma (loan)	37/2
2016-17	Roma	35/0
2017-	Chelsea	149/7

PLAYER 6

NAME ....

BORN		Havlickuv Brod, Czech Republic
DATE OF BIRTH		27 February 1995 (aged 26)

YEARS	CLUB	GAMES/GOALS
2014-20	Slavia Prague	158/40
2015	Viktoria Zizkov (loan)	14/0
2017	Slovan Liberec (loan)	13/0
2020	West Ham (loan)	13/3
2020-	West Ham	41/10

ONCE UPON A TIME...

Reckon you could write an epic footy story? Here's your chance!

WHAT TO DO

1 First of all, you need a cool name for your footy fairytale. Grab a dice and roll it three times to get the three parts of your title.

2 Once you know the title, you can start to think about your story.

3 Follow our top tips before beginning to write your very own footy fairytale!

PART 1

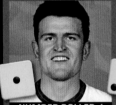
NUMBER ROLLED 1
HARRY MAGUIRE

NUMBER ROLLED 2
JURGEN KLOPP

NUMBER ROLLED 3
MASON MOUNT

NUMBER ROLLED 4
DECLAN RICE

NUMBER ROLLED 5
SEAN DYCHE

NUMBER ROLLED 6
RAHEEM STERLING

AND THE

PART 2

NUMBER ROLLED 1
SWASHBUCKLING PIRATES OF

NUMBER ROLLED 2
CURIOUS CREATURES OF

NUMBER ROLLED 3
DASTARDLY DINOSAURS OF

NUMBER ROLLED 4
BIG BAD BEAR OF

NUMBER ROLLED 5
WILD THINGS OF

NUMBER ROLLED 6
NINJA DOGS OF

PART 3

NUMBER ROLLED 1
THE LOST KINGDOM

NUMBER ROLLED 2
VULTURE VOLCANO

NUMBER ROLLED 3
SKELETON ISLAND

NUMBER ROLLED 4
BURNLEY TOWN CENTRE

NUMBER ROLLED 5
THE EERIE FOREST

NUMBER ROLLED 6
LONDON ZOO

WRITE YOUR BOOK TITLE HERE .... **PART 1** .... **AND THE** .... **PARTS 2 & 3** ....

HERE ARE SOME TOP TIPS ON HOW TO WRITE YOUR STORY!

THE CHARACTERS
- Who is your hero?
- Who is the villain?
- What are their names?
- What do they look like? Try to paint a picture of them with words!
- How do you want the reader to feel about them?
- How do they behave?

THE PLOT
- Where is your story going to take place?
- How many different places will your characters go?
- When is the story taking place – in the past, now, or in the future?
- Do you want it to be scary, action-packed, magical, funny – or something else?

MY NOTES

MY NOTES

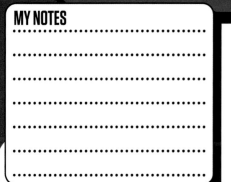

WRITE YOUR BOOK TITLE HERE

THE STORY
- Break it down into a beginning, a middle and an end!
- How will you draw the reader in – to capture their attention straight away and make them desperate to read on?
- How will your story end? Will there be a twist? Will they all live happily ever after?

GETTING STARTED
- Read the first page of some of your favourite books to see how other authors begin their stories.

TOP TIP!
Avoid repeating the same words – use a thesaurus to find alternative words.

MY NOTES

MY NOTES

TURN OVER FOR MORE!

WRITE YOUR BOOK TITLE HERE

....

BY

WRITE YOUR NAME HERE

....

....

....

....

....

....

....

....

....

....

....

....

....

....

....

....

....

....

....

....

....

....

....

....

....

....

....

....

Continue your story on some more paper if necessary!

RONALDO
RONALDO
RONALDO
RONALDO
RONALDO
RONALDO

BRAZIL

98 caps / 62 goals / 3 x FIFA World Player of the Year 2 x Ballon d'Or
Cruzeiro / PSV Eindhoven / Barcelona / Inter Milan / Real Madrid / AC Milan / Corinthians

JAY-JAY OKOCHA

NIGERIA

ARE YOU A

FOOTY GENIUS?

ONE BRAIN-BUSTIN' QUIZ. FOUR DIFFICULTY LEVELS.

| BEGINNER | AMATEUR | PROFESSIONAL | WORLD CLASS |

CAN YOU COMPLETE IT ALL?

LOADING QUIZ...

TURN OVER FOR MORE!

2 POINTS FOR EACH CORRECT ANSWER!
Answers on page 92

1

Which one of these Premier League clubs plays at Goodison Park?

A Burnley | **B** Chelsea | **C** Everton | **D** Wolves

2

Which one of these players was NOT part of England's Euro 2020 squad?

A Jude Bellingham

B Conor Coady

C James Maddison

D Dominic Calvert-Lewin

3

Which Premier League club did Italy boss Roberto Mancini manage from 2009 to 2013?

A Arsenal | **B** Chelsea | **C** Man. City | **D** Liverpool

4

Which club has won the Champions League the most times?

A Liverpool

B Real Madrid

C AC Milan

D Bayern Munich

5

Which of these awesome Premier League stars does NOT play for Brazil?

A Roberto Firmino

B Fred

C Richarlison

D Pedro Neto

MY SCORE ☐ /10

LOADING NEXT LEVEL...

1 Which one of these clubs has never won the Premier League?

A Blackburn   **B** Leicester   **C** Arsenal   **D** Tottenham

2 Which one of these players has won the Premier League Golden Boot?

A Romelu Lukaku   **B** Raheem Sterling

C Marcus Rashford   **D** Jamie Vardy

3 Which one of these clubs does NOT come from Italy?

A Atalanta   **B** Torino

C RB Leipzig   **D** Lazio

4 Which of these epic kits was worn by the Spain team during Euro 2020?

A   **B**

C   **D**

5 Which one of these world megastars has scored the most career goals?

A Cristiano Ronaldo

B Edinson Cavani

C Harry Kane

D Lionel Messi

MY SCORE ☐ /10

1

Can you complete this tricky crossword?

ACROSS

5 Jude Bellingham's first club (10)
6 The biggest stadium in Europe (3, 4)
8 Nickname of Crystal Palace, the _____ (6)
9 Host country of Euro 2024 (7)
10 Country of legendary Prem striker, Dimitar Berbatov (8)

DOWN

1 European club that plays at Stade Velodrome (9)
2 Atletico Madrid manager, Diego _____ (7)
3 Chelsea ace who spent 2018-19 on loan at Derby (5, 5)
4 Home of West Ham, _____ Stadium (6)
7 Scotland striker who plays for Southampton (3, 5)

2 Which Football League club plays at this stadium?

A Portsmouth
B Plymouth
C Peterborough
D Preston

3 Which country did this man lead at Euro 2020?

A Sweden
B Denmark
C Austria
D Czech Republic

5 Which club did Gareth Southgate manage from 2006 to 2009?

A Crystal Palace
B Aston Villa
C Middlesbrough
D QPR

4 Which of these stars has the most England caps?

A John Stones
B Harry Maguire
C Jordan Pickford
D Kieran Trippier

MY SCORE ☐ /28

LOADING NEXT LEVEL...

2 POINTS FOR EACH CORRECT ANSWER!
Answers on page 92

1 Which one of these badges belongs to a League One football club?

A Leyton Orient

B Shrewsbury

C Luton

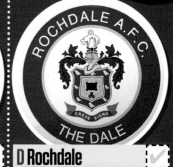
D Rochdale

2 Which one of these four ballers was NOT born in France?

A Riyad Mahrez

B Pierre-Emerick Aubameyang

C N'Golo Kante

D Eduardo Camavinga

3 The two players in this photo are now Prem managers – who are they?

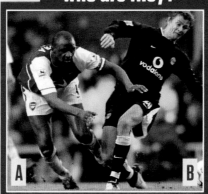
A
B

A _____
B _____

4 Jack Grealish was on loan at which club in 2013-14?

A Bolton

B Walsall

C Swansea

D Notts County

5 Fill in the blanks in these tough UCL sequences below!

A

2020-21	Thomas Tuchel
2019-20	Hansi Flick
2018-19	_____
2017-18	Zinedine Zidane
2016-17	Zinedine Zidane

B

2020-21	Man. City
2019-20	_____
2018-19	Tottenham
2017-18	Liverpool
2016-17	Juventus

C

1	Cristiano Ronaldo	134 goals
2	Lionel Messi	120 goals
3	_____	73 goals
4	Karim Benzema	71 goals
5	Raul	71 goals

MY SCORE ▢ /16

MATCH of the DAY magazine

LUIS

PORTUGAL

FIGO

127 caps / 32 goals / Wing wizard / Sporting Lisbon / Barcelona / Real Madrid / Inter Milan

10 YEARS IN EUROPE

Who's won what over the past decade

		2011-12	2012-13	2013-14	2014-15
	LA LIGA	 Real Madrid	Barcelona	Atlético Madrid	Barcelona
	SERIE A	Juventus	Juventus	Juventus	Juventus
	BUNDESLIGA	 BVB 09	 FC Bayern München	Bayern München	Bayern München
	LIGUE 1	Montpellier	Paris Saint-Germain	Paris Saint-Germain	Paris Saint-Germain
	CHAMPIONS LEAGUE	Chelsea	Bayern München	Real Madrid	Barcelona
	EUROPA LEAGUE	Atlético Madrid	Chelsea	Sevilla	Sevilla
	EUROPEAN GOLDEN SHOE	LIONEL MESSI BARCELONA 50 GOALS	LIONEL MESSI BARCELONA 46 GOALS	LUIS SUAREZ LIVERPOOL CRISTIANO RONALDO REAL MADRID 31 GOALS	CRISTIANO RONALDO REAL MADRID 48 GOALS

PAZ SAYS
A few badges hogging the table here– some clubs need to step up and start getting involved!

2015-16	2016-17	2017-18	2018-19	2019-20	2020-21

...IS SUAREZ BARCELONA	**LIONEL MESSI** BARCELONA	**LIONEL MESSI** BARCELONA	**LIONEL MESSI** BARCELONA	**CIRO IMMOBILE** LAZIO	**ROBERT LEWANDOWSKI** BAYERN MUNICH
...0 GOALS	37 GOALS	34 GOALS	36 GOALS	36 GOALS	41 GOALS

DEL PIERO

ITALY

QUIZ A GROWN-UP!

It's time for you to take on the role of quizmaster now – so grab an adult and put them to the test!

HOW DID THEY DO?
TURN TO p92 FOR THE ANSWERS!

1

Which French club did this England star play for between 1989 and 1992?

CLUB

2 Name this football legend from his profile below!

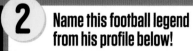

| DATE OF BIRTH | 21 March 1961 (age 60) |
| PLACE OF BIRTH | Erlangen, West Germany |

YEARS	CLUB	GAMES/GOALS
1979–84	B. Monchengladbach	200/51
1984–88	Bayern Munich	150/69
1988–92	Inter Milan	153/53
1992–2000	Bayern Munich	256/31
2000	MetroStars	16/0

NAME

3

A   B

Can you name these two footy hardmen from the 1990s?

PLAYER A

PLAYER B

4 Three Dutch players have won the Premier League Golden Boot – name them all!

PLAYER 1

PLAYER 2

PLAYER 3

5 These four all played for the same Premier League club during the 1992-93 season – name that team!

CLUB

6

A   B

Which two clubs are pictured here battling in the 1987 FA Cup final?

CLUB A

CLUB B

FINAL SCORE	0-3	Epic fail – they need to buy you a serious treat!
/10	4-8	Not bad – but not good enough, grown-up!
	9-10	Sorry, quizmaster – the adult gets control of the TV for the whole day!

10 REASONS TO BE BUZZING FOR EURO 20

Next summer some of the best women's ballers battle it out for European glory – and we can't wait!

1 IT'S IN ENGLAND!

After the epic drama we saw at Wembley and Hampden Park during Euro 2020, we're super excited that Euro 2022 is happening in England. Games take place in July across the country, from Sheffield to Southampton. The opening game will be played at Old Trafford and the final is at Wembley!

WEMBLEY

OLD TRAFFORD

2 GREAT GOALSCORERS!

One thing we'll 100% see at the Euros is goals. So many on-fire forwards will be there, including the Netherlands' record goalscorer Vivianne Miedema and Spain star Jenni Hermoso, who bagged six goals in seven UCL games this season. There's so much talent!

MIEDEMA

This is going to be the best Euros ever!

22!

THE TEAM TO BEAT

3 GERMAN DOMINANCE!

Germany are the team to beat, as they've won eight out of the last ten Euros titles. Only Norway and the Netherlands have lifted the trophy other than Germany since 1989. We're pumped to see who steps up to claim the trophy this time around!

4 ENGLAND STARS!

The Lionesses will have a squad stacked with skill, but their form in the run-up to the competition hasn't been great. New Lionesses boss Sarina Wiegman won Euro 2017 with the Netherlands, so she'll be hoping to get the best out of elite talent like Lucy Bronze to win another!

WHITE

GREENWOOD

HANSEN

5 BARCA'S BEST!

Spanish giants Barcelona dominated the Women's Champions League last season, and they have plenty of players going to Euro 2022. Most will be playing for Spain, but we can't wait to see how forward Caroline Graham Hansen gets on for outsiders Norway!

TURN OVER FOR MORE!

6 ALL NEW FOR NI!

They're the only team making their Euros debut in 2022, but Northern Ireland are ready to spring some shocks. They fought hard to get past Ukraine in a Euros play-off, despite injury to top goalscorer Rachel Furness, and will be aiming to make some history in England!

NORTHERN IRELAND

CASCARINO

HARDER

7 PERFECT PLAYMAKERS!

The tournament will see some of the game's top creators fight for the gold! Chelsea's Pernille Harder wants to push her Denmark team to better their second-place finish at Euro 2017, while Germany's epic Dzsenifer Marozsan and France's Delphine Cascarino have the tek to set the pitch on flames!

KELLY

TOONE

BUHL

8 NEW HEROES!

Summer tournaments are the perfect place to see new stars born. We all know how great England ballers Chloe Kelly and Ella Toone are, but Euro 2022 could be their moment to break out on the big stage. Watch out for Germany's pacy and skilful Klara Buhl, too!

9 IT'S ON THE BBC!

Yes, that's right! Don't worry if you can't get down to a game – the BBC will be covering the whole event, so you can watch live matches and keep up to date with everything else that you don't want to miss!

HOUGHTON

NETHERLANDS

10 FINALS FULL OF GOALS!

Instead of boring 1-0 wins, we've seen some absolute goal-fests in past finals. In 2009, England reached the final only for Germany to hammer them 6-2, while the last final in 2017 saw the Netherlands beat Norway 4-2. They very rarely disappoint!

Watch Euro 2022 live on the BBC next summer!

QUIZ ANSWERS!

Man. United lost to Villarreal in the Europa League final!

WHO IS OLDER?
From p9

1 Cristiano Ronaldo
2 Rihanna
3 Jurgen Klopp
4 Taylor Swift
5 Holly Willoughby
6 Ariana Grande

MY SCORE ANSWER **OUT OF 6**

THE COUNTRY QUIZ!
From p59

1 A, 2 C, 3 C, 4 B, 5 B, 6 B, 7 C,
8 B, 9 A

MY SCORE ANSWER **OUT OF 9**

A YEAR IN FOOTBALL!
From p69

1 A, 2 A, 3 C, 4 C, 5 B,
6 B, 7 B, 8 A, 9 C

MY SCORE ANSWER **OUT OF 9**

Tyrone Mings started out in non-league footy!

GUESS WHO!
From p71

PLAYER 1 Tyrone Mings
PLAYER 2 Dominic Calvert-Lewin
PLAYER 3 Che Adams
PLAYER 4 Diogo Jota
PLAYER 5 Antonio Rudiger
PLAYER 6 Tomas Soucek

MY SCORE ANSWER **OUT OF 6**

ARE YOU A FOOTY GENIUS?
From p77

Beginner
1 C, 2 C, 3 C, 4 B, 5 D
Amateur
1 D, 2 D, 3 C, 4 D, 5 A
Pro

2 C, 3 B, 4 A, 5 C
World class
1 B, 2 D, 3 Patrick Vieira and Ole Gunnar Solskjaer, 4 D,
5 A Jurgen Klopp, B PSG,
C Robert Lewandowski

MY SCORE ANSWER **OUT OF 64**

Chris Waddle won three French titles with Marseille!

QUIZ A GROWN UP!
From p87

1 Marseille
2 Lothar Matthaus
3 John Fashanu and Vinnie Jones
4 Ruud van Nistelrooy, Jimmy Floyd Hasselbaink, Robin van Persie
5 Liverpool
6 Coventry and Tottenham

MY SCORE ANSWER **OUT OF 10**

MATCH of the DAY

Write to us at...

Match of the Day magazine
Immediate Media, Vineyard House,
44 Brook Green, Hammersmith,
London, W6 7BT

Telephone 020 7150 5513

Email inbox@motdmag.com

Match of the Day mag editor	Mark Parry
Deputy editor	Lee Stobbs
Senior art editor	Blue Buxton
Senior designer	Bradley Wooldridge
Annual designers	Al Parr, Pete Rogers
Writer	Jake Wilson
Group picture editor	Natasha Thompson
Picture editor	Jason Timson
Production editor	Neil Queen-Jones
Editorial director	Corinna Shaffer
Annual images	Getty Images

BBC Books an imprint of Ebury Publishing 20 Vauxhall Bridge Road London SW1V 2SA. BBC Books is part of the Penguin Random House group of companies whose addresses can be found at global.penguinrandomhouse.com. Copyright © Match Of The Day magazine 2021. First published by BBC Books in 2021 www.penguin.co.uk. A CIP catalogue record for this book is available from the British Library. ISBN 9781785946783. Commissioning editor: Albert DePetrillo; project editor: Daniel Sorensen; production: Phil Spencer. Printed and bound in Italy by Elcograf S.p.A. The authorised representative in the EEA is Penguin Random House Ireland, Morrison Chambers, 32 Nassau Street, Dublin D02 YH68 Penguin Random House is committed to a sustainable future for our business our readers and our planet. This book is made from Forest Stewardship Council ® certified paper.

BBC

The licence to publish this magazine was acquired from BBC Studios by Immediate Media Company on 1 November 2011. We remain committed to making a magazine of the highest editorial quality one that complies with BBC editorial and commercial guidelines and connects with BBC programmes.

Match Of The Day Magazine is is published by Immediate Media Company London Limited under licence from BBC Studios. © Immediate Media Company London Limited 2021.

MATCH of the DAY

STERLING

CUTHBERT

KANE

LEGENDS LOVE MOTD MAG!

ALEXANDER-ARNOLD

RASHFORD

JAMIE VARDY

THE UK'S No.1 FOOTY MAG!

2022 FOOTY BINGO!

This bingo thing isn't just for your grandparents to play with all their ancient mates – **MOTD** mag's version is fun for everyone!

THE RULES Tick each square as it happens in 2022 – and see how many you have filled in at the end of the year!

PAZ TRIES A NEW HAIRCUT!

THE REF FORGETS HIS CARDS!

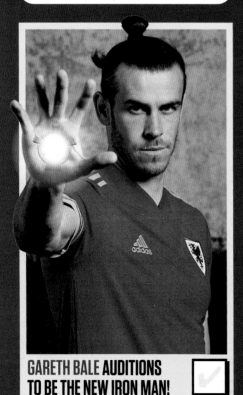

GARETH BALE AUDITIONS TO BE THE NEW IRON MAN!

KALVIN PHILLIPS SWAPS FOOTY FOR BASKETBALL!